Chagford

of Yesteryear

Chips Barber

OBELISK PUBLICATIONS

OTHER TITLES IN THIS SERIES

Ashburton of Yesteryear, *John Germon & Pete Webb*
The Teign Valley of Yesteryear, Parts I and II, *Chips Barber*
Brixham of Yesteryear, Parts I, II and III, *Chips Barber*
Pinhoe of Yesteryear, Parts I and II, *Chips Barber*
Princetown of Yesteryear, Parts I and II, *Chips Barber*
Kingsteignton of Yesteryear, *Richard Harris*
Heavitree of Yesteryear, *Chips Barber*
Kenton and Starcross of Yesteryear, *Eric Vaughan*
Exmouth Century, Parts One and Two, *George Pridmore*
Ide of Yesteryear, *Mavis Piller*
Exmouth of Yesteryear, *Kevin Palmer*
Sampford Peverell of Yesteryear, *Bridget Bernhardt & Jenny Holley*
Sidmouth of Yesteryear, *Chips Barber*
St Thomas of Yesteryear, Parts I and II, *Mavis Piller*
Whipton of Yesteryear, *Chips Barber & Don Lashbrook*
Beesands and Torcross of Yesteryear, *Cyril Courtney*
Dawlish of Yesteryear, *Chips Barber*
Devon's Railways of Yesteryear, *Chips Barber*
Kingskerswell of Yesteryear, *Chips Barber & John Hand*
Torquay of Yesteryear, *Leslie Retallick*
Dartmoor of Yesteryear, *Chips Barber*
Okehampton of Yesteryear, *Mike and Hilary Wreford*
Lympstone of Yesteryear, *Anne Scott*

OTHER TITLES ABOUT THIS AREA

The Great Little Chagford Book, *Chips Barber*
Walks in the Chagford Countryside, *Terry Bound*
We have over 180 Devon titles; for a current list please send SAE to
Obelisk Publications, 2 Church Hill, Pinhoe, Exeter EX4 9ER

Acknowledgements

I would like to express my thanks to the ever-helpful Mr & Mrs Colin Smith of Bowden's, Chagford, for allowing me to copy a handful of pictures housed in their shop's museum; to the marvellous Mavis Piller, who provided a couple of important pictures; and to the long-defunct firm of Jerome Dessain (and to Nicholas Toyne who isn't!) for page 27 bottom. All the other pictures are from my own collection.

First published in 2002 by
Obelisk Publications, 2 Church Hill, Pinhoe, Exeter, Devon
Designed and Typeset by Sally Barber
Printed in Great Britain
by Colour C Ltd, Devon

Chagford

of Yesteryear

There is no place quite like Chagford! Where else in Devon would you find such a good range of shops, public houses and hotels in so small a place so far from the sea? This little book portrays the delights of Chagford, and those of the immediate district, largely through the work of the postcard photographers of the past.

In his book *A History of Devonshire* (1886), R. N. Worth wrote: *For many a long year Chagford seems to have steadily thriven, and to have developed a sturdy independence of character that its comparative isolation on the borders of Dartmoor greatly helped to maintain. Within a very few years it was the quaintest of all the moorland centres; but its greater accessibility as a summer resort has hopelessly modernized its leading features. Nor is this to be wondered at. So delightful are its surroundings in the summer-time, and so proud are the natives of its attractions, common rumour avers that if a Chagford man is then asked where he lives, his sharp retort is, "Chagford, and what do you think?" But in winter, so depressed is he by the change of conditions, the rejoinder will be "Chaggyford, good Lord!" The joke is an old one, but an apt illustration of the sharply contrasted conditions of the moorland climate.*

Taken from a point close to Rushford Tower, this view shows the town dwarfed by two towering hills, Nattadon to the left, and the impressive Meldon to the right. It was on the slopes of the latter that a most peculiar golf course opened on 8 June 1908. High on the steep slopes golfers battled against the forces of gravity; in addition they had to contend with the frequent frustration of losing golf balls in the deep vegetation on the common land.

The golf course was effectively replaced by the one at the Manor House, shown above, in the parish of North Bovey, about three miles from Chagford. The Rt Hon W. H. Smith, who founded the well-known chain of shops, had strong connections with the neighbouring Moretonhampstead district. His son, who became Viscount Hambleden, was responsible for building the huge Manor House. The Great Western Railway acquired it in 1927 and a few years later employed J. W. Abercrombie, a well-known golf-course architect, to design a course on its 200 acres of parkland. If you look closely at this picture, which looks westwards from near North Bovey, you may be able to make out the peak of Kestor Rock rising above the hotel, whilst to the right is a distant Meldon Hill.

Fishermen were also attracted to the Chagford area, the clear, well-oxygenated rivers being ideal for game fishing. But the waters had to be properly managed. This article appeared in the *Western Times* on 18 June 1869:

FISHING IN THE TEIGN Means are being taken to secure the protection of fishing in the Teign between Steps Bridge and Dartmoor, distance twelve miles. At an influential meeting of landowners held a few days ago, a committee was appointed to report on the subject. There were present – The vicar of Chagford (Rev H. G. Hames) who presided, Messrs J. Drewe (Powderham), N. G. Bragg, T. T. Coniam, J. Ponsford, R. L. Berry, J. N. Stevenson, J. Hooper, R. Aggett (Three Crowns, Chagford), Pollard, R. Stanbury, R. Thorn and J. Tarr. The chairman read the rules of the proposed association, as agreed

by the committee: 1st – That members be allowed to fish in the river from the 1st of March to the 30th September, both days inclusive. 2nd – That an application be made to the Quarter Sessions to appoint additional conservators for the upper part of the Teign. 3rd – That the river be preserved from the end of the Duchy rights to Steps Bridge. 4th – That owners and occupiers who give up their right of water to the association have tickets free of cost. 5th – That only fair rod and line fishing be permitted. 6th – That no wading be allowed, and that the committee use their utmost endeavours with the owners and occupiers to have the bushes cut down, as they (the committee) deem necessary. 7th – Any person holding a ticket, and not complying with these rules it shall be forfeited. 8th – That the affairs of the association be managed by a committee, consisting of Messrs Ponsford, Berry, Bragg, Gregory, Coniam, Clarke, Barrington, Hooper (Withecombe), Nash, Pollard, and Revs Ingle and Cornish, and that three form a quorum. 9th – That no dog be permitted to accompany a member. 10th – That two meetings shall be held

annually at Moreton, and no fresh rules be made except at one of these meetings, or at a special meeting when fourteen days' notice must be sent to each member. 11th – That the subscription for the season be 10s 6d each, and daily tickets 1s. 12th – That no keeper be allowed to fish. 13th – That two keepers be appointed to watch the river. Mr Hames added that the committee thought that it would not be practicable, at present, to issue tickets for fishing. They felt assured that at this time of the year fish were greatly destroyed by nets and other modes of fishing, and he would therefore suggest that notices should be posted near each bridge – and there were ten bridges between Steps Bridge and Dartmoor – cautioning persons against wading, groping [fish!], using any net, line, night-hook, or catching fish in any other illegal manner on the water belonging to the Upper Teign Association, and that if they were so found they would be prosecuted; that the committee already appointed be requested to act until the next meeting; that the Earl of Devon be appointed chairman, Sir H. R. Ferguson Davie, Bart MP, vice-chairman; that the consideration of the rules submitted by the committee be adjourned until the next meeting, to be held in January, 1870. He did not consider there would be any objection to these rules or the suggestions he had thrown out, inasmuch as they did not interfere with the rights or the liberties of anyone, their only object being to protect the fishing of the river.

So who was the prime influence in the genesis of Chagford as an inland resort in Victorian times? Although originally from Wiltshire, the Hames family became well established at Chagford. Succeeding his father as Rector in 1852, the Rev H. G. Hames was just one of a long line of clergy from this family to serve the ancient stannary town. To quote an early-days version of the local guide-book: *He was our "Kingsley": he planned a modern drainage system, brought to the town a supply of pure water to replace the "Town Lake" which hitherto had provided at one and the same time both drinking water and a drain! He formed a gas company in 1869 and in 1889 an electricity company which used the water power of the old woollen mill to provide light for the houses and streets of the town, thus becoming the first place west of London to have electricity for street lighting. The Reading Room and the Library were also the result of his efforts; and his love of music gave his parishioners the joy of Handel on Sundays and a brass band on weekdays!*

Colville George Hayter-Hames was the only son of the above. Born in 1859, he was a man of many talents. In 1894 he became the first chairman of the Chagford Parish Council. Like his father he was a fine musician; frequently he and fellow family members took part in local concerts. Although he didn't marry until he was 38 years old, he fathered two sons. Sadly, 23-year-old Noel Hayter-Hames was killed in action in India in 1925; the screen in the church was erected to his memory. When Colville George passed away at the age of 69, in August 1928, his obituary in the local press ran to a full page.

Greenacres was just one of a large number of hotels in or near Chagford. Its advertisement was quick to point out that it was 'on a sheltered hillside' (out of the wind) and that it 'faced south' (enjoyed a sunny aspect). Just 'three minutes from village', it listed the nearby amenities of 'riding, fishing, swimming, bowls, golf and tennis'. In addition to all this, it had 'bedside lamps in all bedrooms'. Whatever next?

As will be seen, this property once traded under a different name. In *The Come to Devon Guide*, published years earlier, this picture was accompanied by the following text: *Mrs Webb, Ferndale, Chagford, Board Residence and Apartments. Thoroughly comfortable. South and West aspects. Very bright and sunny. Garden and Meadow in front.*

Five minutes from Post Office and Buses. Liberal Table. A close look will reveal a few subtle changes between the two images.

The Beverley Private Hotel was yet another establishment to offer comfortable accommodation to visitors. This was the wording which featured in its advertisement:

Unrivalled situation facing south with panoramic views of the Moors and Upper Teign Valley. A comfortable homely hotel where guests' needs are studied and every effort made to make the holiday a memorable one. Own poultry, fruit and vegetables, resident proprietors Major & Mrs T. G. Hughes. They were the parents of Alwyn Hughes, who later became Mrs Rolf Harris. Apparently, if there were no rooms available within the hotel, the Australian artist would pitch a tent on the lawn, Chagford's equivalent of the 'outback'!

Below (and opposite) is the Moor Park Hotel, where 'All beds are aired regularly'.

According to a past advertisement, The Globe Hotel *is the oldest hostelry in Chagford... Every comfort. All motor bus services pass the door, and will drop or take up passengers.* Certainly parking wouldn't have been a problem in those days! The advertisement to the left of the front door is for Dartmoor Coaching Trips.

The picture postcard to the right shows a scene of quiet contentment in the 'Bar, Ye Olde Globe Inn'. An elderly gentleman relishes a drop of ale whilst his dogs enjoy the warmth and glow of a blazing fire.

The view below shows the Toby Jug Café, which had a juke-box in the 1960s. It is now a restaurant, its name reflecting its address, 22 Mill Street.

In the centre of the bottom picture opposite is the former Moorlands Hotel. In the 1950s, it included this as part of the wording for its advertisement: *Moorlands Hotel, Chagford, On the borders of Dartmoor. Famous as a Health Resort, for its beautiful scenery and sporting facilities. Offers great attraction to visitors, who are well catered for at the "Moorlands Hotel," which is pleasantly situated in its own grounds, including Hard Tennis Court and Croquet Lawn, commanding glorious views for miles. Central for walks, drives, motor tours, hunting, fishing, golf, etc. Own Farm and Dairy Produce. Chauffeur and Self-Drive Cars for Hire. Proprietor: R. Lloyd Hill, Licensed, All bedrooms with hot and cold running water. Private Bathrooms. Central Heating. Garages for 16 Cars.*

Here is an article from 1862 which sheds some light on the origin of The Market House. *Many of our readers will doubtless remember a small, low, thatched building in the Market-place at Chagford; the sides were in part open, in part closed with stonework, in part with wood, and large folding doors were prominent features. We used the word "were" as this building has disappeared and a new Market-house is in the course of erection from the designs of Mr Herbert Williams of London, liberally presented by him to the subscribers of this building. The interesting event to the inhabitants of Chagford of laying the North-east corner stone took place on Monday, July 28th, when that duty was undertaken and most ably performed by Mrs Hames, the wife of the worthy rector of the parish. At noon the first signs of the approaching event were heard by the enlivening strains of the Chagford band, which then took up its position, and the persons who were to take part in the ceremony then assembled round the spot on which the stone was to be laid. The proceedings were opened by Mr G. W. Ormerod, who stated that he believed all that could be said in favour of their departed acquaintance was that it had disappeared covered with years; but that for its actual merits nothing could for some time past be advanced...*

Mr Ormerod then placed on a hollow of the lower stone a glass tube containing photographic views of the old market-house, and a list of the parish officers and building committee. This being covered with a metal plate, Mrs Hames was presented with a

trowel, with which she spread the mortar; the stone then slowly descended as the band played the National Anthem. The Rev H. G. Hames, having applied the square to the stone, and responded to the proper question, 'that he had applied the square and the workmen had done their duty,' then addressed the meeting: They were met to lay the foundation stone of a new Market-house which, when finished, he felt sure would be a great ornament to the place. They could all recollect the unsightly appearance of the old one, and had it not been for the perseverance of some of the local gentlemen they would have had to look at it the rest of their days. He thought the success of the present undertaking was, in the first instance, due to Mr W. Hooper, the active parish churchwarden, but it had been mainly carried through by the untiring energy of Mr Berry, supported by Mr Hooper, Mr Coniam, and Mr Ormerod; and he thought that great credit was especially due to Mr Berry. He considered that when finished the building would not only be ornamental but useful; that it would comprise all requisites of a market-house, and besides those a room for parish meetings and a literary institute,

which, if properly carried out, would promote an intellectual taste among the young people of Chagford, and teach them there was a better and pleasanter way of passing the long winter evenings than in wasting their precious time in the public-houses... They would see from it how much a small place like Chagford could accomplish... It was a fact that they had only received contributions towards the Market-house from those connected with the place, and thus he hoped that generations to come might point at the elegant little structure they had just commenced, and say it was a memorial of the good and friendly feeling which existed throughout the parish in 1862. Mr R. L. Berry and Mr W. Hooper, the churchwardens, then applied the level and plumb-rule and responded "That the workmen had done their duty". This completed, Mrs Hames finished the work by taking the mallet, giving the stone three knocks, and pronouncing "That the stone was truly laid." Mr R. L. Berry, the hon secretary to the building committee, then addressing Mrs Hames, said: That on the part of the subscribers and committee of management he thanked her for having kindly completed the pleasing duty of laying the corner-stone... Three cheers were then cordially given for Mrs Hames and the ladies, and these were followed by cheers for the rector, the churchwardens, the lord of the manor, and Mr Ormerod. The band then struck up a lively march, and the meeting, the largest that has for many years taken place in Chagford, then dispersed.

The 'controversial' Chagford Senior Council School opened for business on 2 October 1936. There had been much discontent at Moretonhampstead over the choice of site (i.e. Chagford) but the local authority believed this to be the most practical place to serve five extensive parishes. Described as 'one of the most modern and up-to-date schools in the West Country', it was opened by Sir Francis Acland, shown above being presented with a silver key by Mr H. V. de C. Hague, the County Architect. There was also a short service conducted by the Rev Cecil F. J. Holmes, rector of Chagford, and the Rev A. C. Phillips, the local Methodist minister.

Chairman of Devon Education Committee, Sir Francis was also called upon to plant a tree to commemorate the event. Here he is shown putting his back into the task with the able assistance of two of the school's pupils.

For many years Mr A. Jewels was headmaster of this secondary school. The school always sought to be practical and gardening was given an important place on the curriculum. According to a report of April 1937: *When the County Council purchased the field in which the school has been built, they arranged that suitable portion of it should be set apart as the school garden. In this the scholars have made great progress in the work of digging and planting, and it is hoped that in time enough vegetables will be grown to meet the daily demand of the three penny dinners. Leading to the school, too, is an avenue including trees presented by the several villages from which the children attend school. Boys in the carpentry section are engaged in making wooden squares to place near each tree recording the name of the donor and the date of planting.*

The 'Good Life' eventually came to an end. The education authority decided that it wasn't a viable proposition to maintain such a school, so it was closed. After a period of adaptation, when it was out of use, it was reopened as a primary school in 1971. Now pupils of secondary-school age have a long journey in order to continue their studies.

Below we have the school staff of the 1950s. According to a note on the back of the photograph, they are (left to right): Miss Bibbings (secretary), Connor, Hawarth, Warren, Storey, Ellis, Hill, Jeffries; front row: Taylor, Punchard, Anthony Jewels (Headmaster), Hayes and Nicholson.

Stevens' Garage is no longer with us: the building in New Street has been demolished to make way for the houses built in Stannary Place in 1994. Above and below are two views taken in Lower Street, a thoroughfare with narrow pavements, which has changed little apart from the amount of through traffic: in these two pictures there isn't a vehicle in sight! Unfortunately one cannot still 'Take Courage' here.

The Jubilee Hall was built in memory of King George V and completed in January 1937. Built by public subscription, it cost £2,000. The roof is covered with cedar-wood shingles and protects a hall which measures 50 feet x 40 feet. By my reckoning that makes the original construction work out at a pound per square foot. Many functions, entertainments and meetings have been staged here. This picture postcard is signed by Jan Stewer, the stage-name of a talented man who often performed at Chagford. Born at Woolwich, in London, A. J. Coles came to Devon to be a schoolmaster at Puddington in mid-Devon before taking further teaching posts at Poltimore, near Exeter, and later at Bovey Tracey. However, he had an ambition to entertain, and through his colourful and amusing Devonshire dialect stories, often based on people with whom he came into contact, he achieved his dream. His books are still cherished. He saw out his last years at Pathfinder Village near Tedburn St Mary. He was killed, in his ninetieth year, in a road accident at Ferndown in Dorset, in August 1965.

Below 'There was a big field to meet the Master (Major A. C. Arden) at the opening meeting of Mid-Devon Foxhounds.' The picture dates from early November 1938.

This summer-time aerial view shows the compact heart of roof-top Chagford. To the far right is the tower of the parish church, whilst just to the left of centre is the Market House in The Square, a bus waiting outside in an otherwise traffic-free environment. At

the top of the centre of the photograph is Lower Street. The manner in which the shadows are cast would suggest that it was taken in the early afternoon.

Chagford is blessed by the two best ironmongers' shops in the county. Standing side by side, they are probably the main reason why people are drawn to the Stannary Town to do their shopping. Looking back at past advertisements, the two were probably more

different in their range of goods and services than they are today. "Webbers will have it" was the slogan that topped a full-page advertisement which went on: *Saddlery and Harness: Trunks, Bags and Fancy Leather Goods: Motor Cycles and Cycles – and Repairs: All leading makes supplied: Tyres, Oils and Accessories: Radio Sets: Advice and Estimates Free: Accumulator Station: everything for the House, Garden, Garage, Stable and Estate: Sports Goods for all seasons: Fishing Tackle: Farm Implements: Garden Tools and requisites: Dairy and Poultry Appliances: The Noted House for Cutlery and Tools: Oil and Electric Cooking and Heating Stoves: Aladdin and Tilley Pressure Lamps and Appliances: Newsagents – Papers delivered and posted – Before buying elsewhere – let us quote you.*

WEBBER & SONS
1922

Meanwhile James Bowden & Son accounted for a half-page advertisement: *Established 1862, Agricultural Implement Manufacturers, General and Furnishing Ironmongers, Shoeing and General Smiths, Vulcan Iron Works, Agents for 'Bottogas', Lighting, Heating & Cooking.* Indeed, some of those items are visible in Bowden's museum, found upstairs at the back of the shop. Both Bowden's

and Webber & Sons continue to satisfy the needs of a shopping hinterland which extends well beyond the parish boundaries.

Above is the Moorlands Dairy when it was housed in earlier premises. It has since relocated twice within the town, the most recent move being into what had been for a few years a tourist information centre, trading under the name 'All Found in Devon', as seen below (right). Other businesses have come and gone, as the shop in Mill Street, seen below left, shows.

The Square, Chagford, Devon.

On the left of the picture above is the front end of the bus run by the London & South Western Railway. This was one of the first public rural bus services in the county. The journey from Chagford to Exeter was accomplished in exactly two hours!

Below, 'Happy New Year' wishes are extended from the post office at Chagford.

Post Office. Chagford.

A HAPPY NEW YEAR

Chagford of Yesteryear

This ancient machine was already 30 years old when presented to the local council in about 1869. The picture was taken in 1939, when it had made its last trip in the town's carnival procession and was due to be replaced by a modern trailer pump. A major fire in February 1938, which destroyed three fifteenth-century properties a few miles from the town, probably led to the decision to find a replacement more able to cope with such a disaster. The local press reported that: *When Chagford Fire Brigade was called to a disastrous outbreak which destroyed three centuries-old cottages ... the fire-fighting equipment at their disposal consisted of a manual engine given to the parish by a fire insurance company, and which was conveyed to the spot on a lorry. Three families, consisting of six adults and a young child, were rendered homeless by the destruction of the property, which is known as Old Wall-cottages. The occupants were Miss Harvey and her companion, Miss Parks; Mr and Mrs J. Harrison and their child; and Mr and Mrs George Lee, who had lived there for thirty years. The continuous mewing and scratching of a cat led to the discovery of the outbreak just before midnight, when all the occupants of the cottages were in bed. Mrs Harrison, who lived in the centre cottage, got up to investigate, and found the rear part of her cottage filled with smoke. She roused her husband, and while he attempted to extinguish the flames in a corner of the thatch, Mrs Harrison warned the other occupants of the cottages of their danger. Hurriedly throwing on some clothing, they rushed to aid Mr Harrison.*

A gusty wind was sweeping the whole length of the buildings, and, with the flames eating up the thatch, which was over one foot thick, the blaze rapidly became beyond control. While the Chagford Brigade was proceeding to the scene, helpers assisted in removing as much furniture as possible into the muddy road, and the bulk of the property belonging to the occupants was saved.

Even had they been equipped with modern apparatus, the brigade, who were directed by Captain G. Dicker, would have had no chance in stemming the blaze. As it was, they could do no more than check it to enable as much furniture to be salvaged as possible.

Relays of men, including firemen, policemen and farm workers, spent hours pumping water from a pool made by damming a stream close to the cottages, while others stripped away portions of thatch in vain efforts to stop the progress of the flames. By 6 a.m. the cottages had been reduced to a heap of smouldering ruins.

The Church of St Michael was dedicated on 30 July 1261 by Bishop Walter Branscombe, a man who loved to travel around his diocese visiting country parishes. It was greatly transformed about 1482 when the fine east window of five lights and a Lady Chapel were added. Until 1931 the church appeared to be in a reasonable state of preservation but on Armistice Day, just as the Service of Remembrance was drawing to a close, plaster fell from the ceiling in the Sanctuary. Close inspection revealed that not only had death-watch beetle destroyed all the laths behind the plaster, but also the oaken beams had rotted and become dangerous. The work to repair the entire roof was carried out by Chagford workmen for an outlay of £2,600, with much of the oak wood used originating from within the parish.

In 1854, the famous Victorian guide James Perrott established a 'walkers' shrine' at Cranmere Pool in the heart of the Dartmoor wilderness. He is now buried in the church-yard at Chagford.

Gidleigh has an ancient church, Holy Trinity. Close to it are found the remains of a medieval castle, or fortified manor house, dating back to about 1300.

The Teign is a lovely river which runs for about 30 miles from the heights of northern Dartmoor down to the sea at Teignmouth. It is possible to follow most of its course by road, footpath or bridleway. Its waters have long supplied the famous swimming pool at Chagford. Opened in the mid-1930s, it is the largest outdoor freshwater swimming pool in Devon.

These two pictures were taken 'next door' to the swimming pool. Rushford Mill and Steps was another favourite venue for the postcard photographer.

In a newspaper feature from 8 July 1904, a journalist took the walk which leads from Chagford towards Drewsteignton. This is what he had to say about his excursion: *This leads over the Teign by a bridge, and we soon afterwards turn in through the farmyard of a mill – that sounds rather like a Paddyism, but it is a fact – called Rushford Mill, which belongs to the Rector of Chagford. Getting over a dilapidated stile we follow a path by the river Teign; but, unfortunately for ladies, we soon come to a wood, through which no harm would be done were a decent footpath to be made for the accommodation of visitors; but it is not done.*

The Sandy Park Inn is situated on a crossroads, not far from the River Teign at Sandy Park Bridge, but about a 'country mile' from Chagford. It is rumoured that the lovely Great Tree Hotel, on the Moretonhampstead to Whiddon Down road, started its life as a private residence at Holsworthy in West Devon. It was supposedly moved to its present position when its owners could not bear to leave their old home behind. This is how it looked on a postcard dated 1970.

Spinsters' Rock, Dartmoor's most famous example of a dolmen, has also attracted the attentions of the postcard photographer. It's a place with public access but finding it has proved something of a challenge to the Dartmoor novice. This is how it was featured by R. N. Worth in his book *A History of Devonshire* (1886): *Here stands, on a farm called Shilstone, the only cromlech left in Devon, which once formed the central feature of a group of stone circles and avenues. It fell in January, 1862, and was "restored" in the same year. Though the "quoit" is two feet thick, fifteen in length, and ten in breadth, a builder and a carpenter of Chagford, by the aid of pulleys and a screw-jack, replaced it at a cost of £20; and thus very much reduced the vague wonder that commonly attaches to the erection of such structures. The village tradition is that the "Spinster's Rock," as it is called, was erected by three spinsters one morning before breakfast; and these have been suggested as the Valkyriur.*

Below is the Easton Court, which was developed as a small, quality hotel in the 1920s. It is where Evelyn Waugh wrote his most famous work, *Brideshead Revisited.*

Although it looks ancient, Castle Drogo is a product of the twentieth century. Julius Drewe wanted to live in a castle; although it took twenty years and was scaled down from the original plans, he got what he wanted. Sir Edwin Lutyens was the celebrated architect of this remarkable building situated in a superb position overlooking the Teign Gorge. It is now a National Trust property of immense interest.

The view below, one of the many pictures in this book by the Dawlish-based Chapman & Son, is from the slopes beneath Castle Drogo looking towards Sharp Tor, an outcrop which rises above the deep Teign Gorge.

Opposite is the former Ashplant's Tea Shelter at Fingle Bridge, tel. no. 21! This family-run business evolved over the years into what is now the Anglers' Rest, a superbly located place of refreshment. Fingle Bridge has, understandably, long been a favourite subject for photographers.

We end our look back at *Chagford of Yesteryear* with a picture taken in an extremely quiet High Street looking towards the church. Today, cars park on the left hand side and vehicles that wish to pass along the road have to wait until their route becomes clear. According to the generously proportioned sign, The Three Crowns Hotel then belonged to someone called Payne. In the days of Edwardian sartorial elegance, M. Parsons, the tailor, just right of centre, would have catered for the needs of the more discerning gentleman of fashion. The premises are now occupied by Whiddons, an antique dealer.